Once there were two sisters, Rose and Ivy.

Rose was helpful.

Ivy was lazy.

One day, Rose saw an old woman.
"Please," said the woman. "Will you
sweep my steps?"
"Yes," said Rose.

After Rose swept the steps clean,
the woman gave her a bag.

It was filled with gold!

Rose showed the gold to Ivy.

"I want my own gold," said Ivy.

Ivy went to see the old woman.

"Please," said the woman. "Will you
fix my gate? It squeaks."

"Yes," said Ivy.

But Ivy went to sleep.

When Ivy woke up, she called, "I fixed
the gate. I want my gold!"

12

The woman opened the gate. It still squeaked.

She gave Ivy a bag.

But it was filled with stones!

16